Clark

SO-BZU-554

LASZLO MOHOLY-NAGY

An exhibition organized by the Museum of Contemporary Art and The Solomon R. Guggenheim Museum under a grant from the Graham Foundation for Advanced Studies in the Fine Arts and in cooperation with the Santa Barbara Museum of Art, the University Art Museum at the University of California, Berkeley, and the Seattle Art Museum.

Published by the Museum of Contemporary Art,
Chicago, 1969
Library of Congress Card Catalogue Number 76-88082
All Rights Reserved
Printed in West Germany

Lenders to the Exhibition

Bauhaus-Archiv, Darmstadt
Busch-Reisinger Museum of Germanic Culture, Cambridge, Massachusetts
Mr. and Mrs. Eugene A. Davidson, Chicago
The Detroit Institute of Arts
Mr. and Mrs. Edward Druzinsky, Chicago
Lillian H. Florsheim Foundation for Fine Arts, Chicago
Walter Gropius, South Lincoln, Massachusetts
The Solomon R. Guggenheim Museum, New York
Haags Gemeentemuseum, The Hague
Herron Museum of Art, Indianapolis
Mr. and Mrs. Leonard J. Horwich, Chicago
Mrs. Claudia Imlay, Santa Monica, California
George M. Irwin, Quincy, Illinois
Jewett Arts Center, Wellesley, Massachusetts
Philip Johnson, New York
Galerie Klihm, Munich
Kovler Gallery, Chicago
Marlborough-Gerson Gallery, New York
Mrs. Sibyl Moholy-Nagy, New York
The Museum of Modern Art, New York
New York University Art Collection, New York
Charles W. Niedringhaus, New York
Mrs. Walter Paepcke, Chicago
Mr. and Mrs. Kenneth Parker, Janesville, Wisconsin
Henry Proskauer, New York
Saarland Museum, Saarbrucken
Seattle Art Museum
Mr. and Mrs. Arthur Siegel, Chicago
Mr. and Mrs. Fred Shore, New York
Smith College Museum of Art, Northampton, Massachusetts
Stedelijk van Abbemuseum, Eindhoven
University Art Museum, University of California, Berkeley
Carlos Raúl Villanueva, Caracas
Whitney Museum of American Art, New York
Yale University Art Gallery, Collection Société Anonyme, New Haven, Connecticut

Foreword

■ The last comprehensive exhibition of paintings and sculptures by Laszlo Moholy-Nagy dates back further than today's museum visitors remember. To honor the memory of the artist who had died the year before, The Museum of Non-Objective Paintings, as The Solomon R. Guggenheim Museum then was called, presented a large-scale survey in the early summer of 1947. Now, almost a quarter of a century later, an evaluation of Moholy-Nagy's historic contribution in the light of contemporary scholarship is long overdue. A resurgent interest in Constructivism and related artistic propositions underlines this need. A little over a year ago the Albright-Knox Art Gallery in Buffalo organized an impressive theme show devoted to Constructivism and its heritage. In recently published books, two artists, successors to the Constructivist tradition, interpreted the pioneering efforts from Tatlin to Moholy-Nagy in terms of kinetic art and systems esthetics. A Bauhaus exhibition far exceeding earlier summations in scope has just completed a tour through Europe, where a reawakening of interest in Moholy-Nagy has followed the 1967 exhibition organized by the Stedelijk van Abbemuseum, Eindhoven. Appropriately, the museum originating the present exhibition is located in the city where Moholy-Nagy spent the last nine years of his life and founded the School of Design.

Jan van der Marck
Director, Museum of Contemporary Art

Thomas M. Messer
Director, The Solomon R. Guggenheim Museum

Acknowledgments

■ I have been privileged in securing the cooperation essential to the success of this exhibition. Mrs. Sibyl Moholy-Nagy greeted the idea of a retrospective with enthusiasm; she was a valuable source of information, a generous lender and the contributor of the catalogue essay. Mr. Thomas M. Messer, Director of The Solomon R. Guggenheim Museum took an interest from the beginning, allowed me free choice from that museum's substantial collection of works by Moholy-Nagy, and participated in the organization of this retrospective showing. Mrs. Diane Waldman, the Guggenheim Museum's Assistant Curator, acted as the vital liaison between the collaborating museums; Miss Linda Konheim, Research Fellow, supervised the production of the catalogue.

■ I am grateful to Mr. G. H. Dorr III, Director of the Santa Barbara Museum of Art, Dr. Peter Selz, Director of the University Art Museum at the University of California, Berkeley, and Mr. Thomas Maytham, Associate Director of the Seattle Art Museum, for arranging for showings in their respective museums and thereby gaining wide circulation of Moholy-Nagy's work along the West Coast of the United States.

■ Lenders to the exhibition deserve special thanks and I appreciate their generosity in making loans available for the better part of a year. The Graham Foundation pledged its support early in the planning stages and gave the museum a grant to allow a more complete show and a more substantial catalogue.

■ Numerous individuals have provided me with help, information and advice. I would like to extend my thanks to Miss Alice Adam, Mr. John Entenza, Mrs. Roland Ginzel, Mr. Richard Gray, Mr. Bernard Karpel, Dr. H. H. Klihm, Mr. Jean Leering, Mrs. Walter Paepcke, Mr. Arthur Siegel, Dr. Carlos R. Villanueva and Miss Hannah Weitemeier.

■ The trustees of the Museum of Contemporary Art enthusiastically supported this tribute to Moholy-Nagy. I wish to mention the following members of my staff: Miss Genie Bird and Mrs. Merrill Rosenberg who edited the catalogue with research assistance from Miss Blandina Albright; Mr. David H. Katzive who assisted on the preparation and presentation of the works exhibited; Mrs. M. C. Carr and Mrs. John Mundo who supervised all shipping arrangements.

J. v. d. M.

Laszlo Moholy-Nagy by Vories Fisher, 1945

Biography*

1895 Born in Bacsbarsod, Hungary
1913 Enrolled as law student in University of Buda-
pest. Befriended writers and musicians and con-
tributed to vanguard magazines.
1914 Called into Austro-Hungarian army and sent to
Russian Theatre of War.
1915 While recovering from shell shock, started
making pencil and crayon sketches.
1917 Severely wounded. During convalescence in
Odessa, then in Szeged, began making grease
crayon and watercolor portraits. With four friends
in Szeged, among them Ludwig Kassák, organized an artists' group which called itself "Ma,"
the Hungarian word for "today."
1918 After discharge from the army, returned to Buda-
pest to take bachelor's degree in law. Continued
drawing and painting.
1919 Began to acquaint himself with the work and
ideas of Kasimir Malevich and El Lissitzky. Left
for Vienna in the fall where the "Ma" group un-
dertook the publication of a contemporary art
quarterly *Horizont.*
1920 Moved to Berlin where he devoted himself to
collages in the spirit of the Berlin Dada group
and made his first experiments with photograms,
photographs without a camera.
1921 Met El Lissitzky in Dusseldorf and made a trip
to Paris.
1922 With Ludwig Kassák in Vienna edited the *Buch
Neuer Künstler,* an anthology of modern art and
poetry. Herwarth Walden of Galerie Der Sturm
in Berlin arranged his first exhibition. Walter
Gropius, brought to the gallery by art writer Adolf
Behne, invited Moholy-Nagy to join the faculty
of the Staatliche Bauhaus in Weimar. Attended
Constructivist Conference in Weimar organized
by Theo van Doesburg.
1923 In the spring began teaching at Weimar Bauhaus.
Took charge of metal workshop and succeeded
Johannes Itten in giving the foundation course.
Collaborated with Oskar Schlemmer and others

on murals, ballet and stage designs; engaged in photography, light and color experiments; and worked in typography and lay-out. With Walter Gropius planned, edited and designed the fourteen *Bauhausbücher* while also involving himself with the periodic *Bauhaushefte*.
Described his paintings as "Constructivist" with emphasis shifting from line to colored form.

1925 Moved with the Bauhaus to Dessau.

1927 With J. J. P. Oud and Willem Pijper participated in the founding of avant garde art monthly, *i 10*, edited by A. Müller Lehning in Amsterdam.

1928 Under rising political pressures, resigned from the Bauhaus together with Walter Gropius. Moved to Berlin making a brilliant career for himself as a stage designer for the progressive Stage Opera and the Piscator Theatre until 1933. ("Tales of Hoffmann," 1929; "The Merchant of Berlin," by Walter Mehring, 1929; "Hin und Her," by Hindemith, 1930; "Madame Butterfly," 1931.) Designed exhibitions in Berlin, Brussels and Paris. Interest continued in photograms and documentary films. As a painter he experimented with new materials: neolith, galalith, trolit, colou, rhodoit and finally plexiglas.

1930 Exhibited a light display machine or rotating sculpture with built-in lights at the Internationale Werkbund Ausstellung in Paris. This sculpture, "Lichtrequisit," was the subject of his best known film, "Lichtspiel schwarz-weiss-grau."

1934 Moved to Amsterdam where a large printing company offered him facilities for experiments with color film and photography. Designed display at the Utrecht "Jaarbeurs" for the manufacturers of artificial silk.

1935 Moved to London where he designed the Courtauld exhibit at the Industrial Fair and became an art advisor for Simpson's, the Royal Air Lines and the London Transport. Published three volumes of documentary photography and made a documentary film, "Life of the Lobster." Began to experiment with three-dimensional paintings, using transparent foreground materials which he called "space modulators."

1936 Alexander Korda commissioned him to create the special effects for "The Shape of Things to Come" by H. G. Wells.

1937 Assumed the directorship of the New Bauhaus in Chicago, a school founded by the Association of the Arts and Industries. After a year the sponsoring organization ran into financial difficulties and the school was forced to close down.

1938 Opened his own School of Design on 247 East Ontario Street, Chicago, with most of the New Bauhaus staff. As a designer worked in an advisory capacity for Spiegel, Inc., the Baltimore and Ohio Railroad, the Parker Pen Company and others.

1941 Joined American Abstract Artists. Developed his space modulator into three-dimensional sculpture.

1945 Increased his activity as a painter and produced many paintings, watercolors and ink drawings in a variety of new approaches.

1946 Died of leukemia in Chicago on November 24. At the time of his death he was President of the Institute of Design (formerly called School of Design), then having 680 students in its building on 632 North Dearborn Street.

* Based on biography in catalogue of 1947 Memorial exhibition, organized by The Solomon R. Guggenheim Foundation, and subsequent catalogue biographies. For book-length biography consult Sibyl Moholy-Nagy, *Experiment in Totality*, 2nd Edition, Cambridge, 1969.

One-Man Exhibitions

1922 Galerie Der Sturm, Berlin
1924 Bauhaus Weimar
Galerie Der Sturm, Berlin
1926 Kunsthaus Fides, Dresden
1930 Nationalmuseum, Stockholm
1931 Delphic Studios, New York (photographs)
1932 Abstraction-Création, Paris
1935 Stedelijk Museum, Amsterdam
1936 Brno, Czechoslovakia
1937 London Gallery, London
1939 Renaissance Society, Chicago
1940 Katherine Kuh Gallery, Chicago
1941 Stendahl Art Galleries, Los Angeles
Institute of Design, Chicago
1947 Museum of Non-Objective Paintings, New York
The Art Institute of Chicago
Cyril's Studio Gallery, Detroit
1948 Portland Art Museum, Portland, Oregon
Museum of Fine Arts, Houston
1950 Fogg Art Museum, Cambridge, Massachusetts
Cincinnati Art Museum, Cincinnati
Rose Fried Gallery, New York
Colorado Springs Fine Arts Center,
Colorado Springs
San Francisco Museum of Art, San Francisco
1951 Circle Gallery, Detroit
1952 Galerie Arnaud, Paris
1953 Kunsthaus, Zurich
Galerie Lutz und Meyer, Stuttgart
1956 Kunstkabinett Klihm, Munich
1957 Kleemann Galleries, New York
1959 Kunstkabinett Klihm, Munich
1961 Kunstmuseum, Dusseldorf
New London Gallery, London
Kunsthalle, Mannheim
1962 Kunstkabinett Klihm, Munich
Museum Folkwang, Essen
Galleria Blu, Milan
1964/65 Museum of Modern Art Circulating Exhibition
shown at: Kent State University, Kent, Ohio; Uni-

versity of Manitoba, Winnipeg, Canada; North
Dakota State University, Fargo, North Dakota;
Northern Michigan University, Marquette, Michi-
gan; Ohio State University, Columbus, Ohio;
Erdahl-Cloyd Union, University of North Carolina,
Raleigh, North Carolina; Allen Memorial Art Mu-
seum, Oberlin College, Oberlin, Ohio; Allegheny
College, Meadville, Pennsylvania; University of
North Carolina, Greensboro, North Carolina; State
University College, Cortland, New York; Watson
Art Gallery, Elmira College, Elmira, New York;
State University College, Geneseo, New York
1966 Galerie Klihm, Munich
1967 Stedelijk van Abbemuseum, Eindhoven
Haags Gemeentemuseum, The Hague
Von der Heydtmuseum, Wuppertal
1968 Brandeis University, Waltham, Massachusetts
Marlborough Fine Art Ltd., London

Selected Group Exhibitions

1923 Kestnergesellschaft, Hannover
"Kunst und Technik – eine neue Einheit," Bauhaus and Staatliches Landesmuseum, Weimar
1926 International Exhibition of Modern Art. Arranged
by the Société Anonyme, Brooklyn Museum,
New York
"Grosse Berliner Kunstausstellung," Kron-
prinzenpalais, Berlin
1927 "Tendenzen abstrakter Malerei in Europa,"
Kunsthalle, Mannheim
1929 Galerie Neue Kunst Hans Goltz, Munich
1930 Internationale Werkbund Ausstellung, Paris
1936 Abstraction-Création, Paris
"Cubism and Abstract Art," The Museum of
Modern Art, New York
"Abstract and Concrete," Lefèvre Gallery,
London
1937 "Konstruktivisten," Kunsthaus, Basel
"Constructive Art," London Gallery, London
1939 "Art of Tomorrow," The Solomon R. Guggenheim
Foundation, New York
1950 "Die Maler am Bauhaus," Haus der Kunst, Munich
1953 "Six Artist Teachers in America," The Museum of
Modern Art Circulating Exhibition (until 1956)
1957 IV Bienal, São Paulo
1958 "50 Ans d'Art Moderne," World's Fair, Brussels
1960 "Konkrete Kunst. 50 Jahre Entwicklung," Zuricher
Kunstgesellschaft, Helmhaus, Zurich
"Construction and Geometry in Painting,"
Galerie Chalette, New York
(circulated to Contemporary Arts Center, Cin-
cinnati, The Arts Club of Chicago and Walker Art
Center, Minneapolis, 1961)
"Paths of Abstract Art," Cleveland Museum of
Art
1962 "Painters of the Bauhaus," Marlborough Fine
Art Ltd., London
1964 "Bauhaus. Idee-Form-Zweck-Zeit," Göppinger
Galerie, Frankfurt am Main
1966 "Kunst Licht Kunst," Stedelijk van Abbemuseum,
Eindhoven

"Konstruktive Malerei 1915–1930," Frankfurter
Kunstverein, Frankfurt am Main
1968 "Plus By Minus: Today's Half-Century," Albright-
Knox Art Gallery, Buffalo, New York
"Acquisitions of the 1930's and 1940's," The
Solomon R. Guggenheim Museum, New York
"50 Years Bauhaus," Württembergischer Kunst-
verein, Stuttgart; Royal Academy of Arts, London;
Stedelijk Museum, Amsterdam
"The Machine," The Museum of Modern Art,
New York

Laszlo Moholy-Nagy

Sibyl Moholy-Nagy
New York
March 1969

■ The work of an artist can be interpreted from two angles. It can be read as a record of personal triumphs and tragedies — the sublimation of an individual fate. On a different plane, it testifies to the values and contradictions of an historical epoch — the sublimation of a collective fate. One can see in Picasso's œuvre the fever chart of his passionate involvements, or the transmigration of art from classical *stasis* into relative *dynamis* to which the artist was a mere instrument.

■ Maintaining this dichotomy, a literary record of Moholy-Nagy's personal life has been attempted elsewhere.[1] An introduction to a retrospective exhibition should focus on the time-bound and time-transcending aspects of his work that have survived his physical existence.

■ Constructivism, which emerged in Eastern Europe as a clearly discernible art movement toward the end of the First World War, syncretized the diverse rebellions against the Beaux-Arts tradition characteristic for the first two decades of the 20th century. Cubism inspired the search for simultaneous inside-outside relationships, and Suprematism the supremacy of objectified over self-conscious emotional symbolism. The failure of the Futurists to project their revolutionary awareness of the fourth dimension of motion-time on to the picture plane stimulated experimentation with kinetic light patterns that exploded the picture frame; and Marinetti's Manifesto, eager to replace the Greek goddess with the combustion engine, pointed toward the scientific potential in art. The air was charged with many more currents — Russian *Proletkult,* declaring art a political instrument, Mondrian's religious vision of a society healed of its ills by the equilibration of opposites in line and color, and the crystallization of architecture as luminous sculpture in the designs of the German *Glaskette* movement, headed by Taut and Scharoun.

■ A new generation of commentators heaped invective of "clever eclecticism" on the Constructivists. The liberation from academic standards, so recently achieved, resulted in an historical amnesia of art criticism which ever since has made the ferreting out of "influences" a deadly game. Yet it was Raphael, Ruysdael, Jongkind, and Turner who produced Renoir and Monet; and Monet, Cezanne, Derain, and Braque who in turn produced Mondrian. It takes a long in-formed vista to realize that the importance of a new creative development rests not on its origins but on the extent to which it surpasses them. Constructivism lifted the innovations of diverse and isolated groups to the status of a genuine and still active revolution be-cause it fulfilled the two prerequisites that distinguish dissent from radical change. It assumed responsibility for all consequences of its new vision, and it proposed a new ethics to replace convictions that had become meaningless. In assuming responsibility, the Construc-tivists took on the entire range of designed environ-ment — "from an ink bottle label to a new city," from theatre, film, dance, and graphics to the reform of visual education from Kindergarten to the involvement of every adult "willing to see."

■ The new ethics that went with the assumption of totality was inextricably connected with the social revolution that swept Europe at the end of the First World War. It rejected Soviet Bolshevism as a new coercive tyranny, and dedicated itself passionately to

the forces of evolution which have produced science, civilization and social systems ... The new dimension of constructivism has no other purpose than to partici-pate in life.[2]

Constructivist ethics did not liquidate the artist. It committed him, by virtue of his specific talent, to teach new vision to all men.

■ It is in the nature of the evolution of function to be transient because each solution is devaluated by the next one. A contemporary chair reveals only to the specialist the genesis from Thonet to Breuer, Mies van der Rohe, Le Corbusier, and Eames. This is even more evident in the curricular development of visual educa-

tion. The ubiquitous Basic Design courses of today have totally absorbed Froebel's *Gifts,* van Doesburg's didactic transfiguration of a cow, and the Bauhaus *Grundlehre.* The evolution of an art form — music, architecture, painting, sculpture — is something else. It remains visible because each realization is a self-reflecting facet in a larger crystal, impervious to the destructive power of obsolescence. Constructivism, dedicated to the *Gesamtkunstwerk,* has left in its art works a permanent record that runs parallel to the functionalist application of its principles.

■ In a letter to his friend Kalivoda,[3] Moholy-Nagy tried to rationalize his continued preoccupation with easel painting, although he had been the most eloquent prophet of a new age in which paint and brushes would be discarded, museums would be closed, and every-one would participate in "painting with light" by tech-nological means on clouds, reflecting and warped sur-faces, photographic emulsion, and architectural vol-umes. Blaming reactionary industry and profit-greedy mass-media for blocking experimentation, and so depriving the masses of "direct contact with the new forces of artistic creation," he concluded:

Since it is impossible at present to realize our dreams of the fullest development of optical techniques (light architecture), we are forced to retain the medium of easel painting.[3]

To the historian the simultaneity of traditional and in-novative visual means seems as natural and inevitable as the coexistence of books and television, ships and space rockets, scholars and computers. Easel painting will always remain the catalyst that precipitates visual changes while remaining constant in its basic concep-tion and function. As long as man builds walls there will be painting, just as long as there will be individual sculpture as long as man designs spaces.

■ The formulation of the Constructivist message in Moholy's lifework can be traced through three stages, each retaining the gains of the previous one while establishing a new ascendancy. A very brief apprenticeship under Cubist influences led to the first plateau of visual independence: *Space objectified and defined by metric lines.* This was followed by: *Chromatic Fundamentalism, developing toward superimpositions.* The concluding stage belonged to: *Light as a reflective and kinetic element in environmental relationships.* His entire work was unified by a commitment to the integrity of materials and processes, and by the intangible and indispensable ingredient of talent.

■ The first phase of Moholy's development grew out of his discovery of the industrial world from which his generation expected redemption from the ignorance and exploitation of rural feudalism.

The art of Moholy-Nagy proclaims the world of man who has become master of the machine ... From railroad landscapes with the powerful diagonals of inclined smoke-stacks rise massive tectonic syntheses of precipitous supporting and tensioning forces. Structural elements are liberated from expediency and practical relativity. They rise to the significance of a self-purposive, self-expressive visual order.[4]

Perspective space receded more and more. The picture plane turned into a projection of "auxiliary lines in places where ordinarily no lines are used — a rhythmic interweaving showing not so much the objects as my excitement about them." Looking at these landscapes and portraits, dated between 1917 and 1920, one is reminded of a passage from the writings of Leonardo da Vinci:

The air is filled with an infinite number of lines, straight and radiating, intercrossing and waving together, without ever coinciding; and they represent for every object the reason of its true form.[5]

■ An "unconscious sense of order" directed Moholy next to the collage. The emotional interaction of planar space and line gained contrast by primary colors in linear elements, organizing space segments. Each made a specific contribution to the harmony of the whole.

Color, which I had so far considered mainly for its illustrative possibilities, was transformed into a force loaded with potential space articulation.[6]

Space was pure object — not the Euclidian container of the object nor the void between parallel lines extending toward infinity, but *das Ding an sich.*

■ Moholy's expanding imagination soon was stopped short by the creative limitations of the collage. He could either refine his orthogonal space harmonies to a precision that must become repetitive; or he could fall into the trap of the later Cubists and early Surrealists by loading his objectified space with *trompe-l'œil* effects which imitated or persiflaged illusionistic painting. Beset by a compulsive visual curiosity, he tried both. The collages composed during his intense friendship with Kurt Schwitters, the Dadaist, abound in *objets trouvés*, cryptic lettering, and social allusions. The last collages, done in his early Bauhaus years, seem abstracts of his paintings, the way a skeleton represents the pure structure of man without the distracting accidence of personal characteristics.

■ The exploration of primary color and line became the basis for the second phase of Moholy's lifework: chromatic fundamentalism. The pure color contrasts of the collages were translated into painting from which evolved the superimpositions that established a personal unduplicable style. From circa 1922 onwards color equals form in a distinctly different vision from the guiding color lines of the first phase. This development marks Moholy's break with Russian Constructivism. As point one in a five-point rejection of all traditional art forms, the brothers Naum Gabo and Antoine Pevsner had declared in their brilliant *Realistic Manifesto:*

We reject in painting: Color as a pictorial element. Color is the idealized optical face of objects, the ex-

ternal and superficial impression of them. Color is accidental and has nothing in common with the inner content of the body.[6]

There is something peculiarly provincial in this statement, as if it were still essential to fight Impressionism, oblivious of Cezanne's chromatic building blocks and van Gogh's color x-rays. Model (modulus) means a small measure of a larger magnitude. Moholy's colors were neither a surface coating of pictorial realism, nor abstract experiments in color theory. They were models of visual fundamentals inherent in nature, small models of the "naturalistic" spectrum and its infinite compositional options.

■ Colors having achieved the role of *dramatis personae* made any descriptive titles impossible. The simplest way to disassociate the spectator's perception from any symbolic contents was the use of serial numbers as picture designations. Until approximately 1925 there is a fairly clear sequence. "A" separates oil paint on canvas from oil on any number of metal or synthetic surfaces which received abbreviations of trade names: Al for aluminium, Gal for galalith, Sil for silverith, etc. It is a nice sidelight on the resistance to total rationality in art that Moholy's serial system soon broke down. There appear cryptic Z's and R's quite out of order, indicating personal associations which remained the painter's secret. Only after he had reached Chicago in 1937 does CH become a steadily maintained prefix which was replaced by the tragic Leu (leukemia) in the last year of his life (fall 1945/fall 1946).

■ Sculpture, however, was another matter and exempt from serialization. It explains the peculiar role played by three-dimensional construction in Moholy's work.

■ It would be impossible spatially and redundant verbally to repeat here Moholy's own moving and concise description of his work with moulded plastics in *Abstract of an Artist.*[7] The decisive point is the function of a three-dimensional composition as environmental medium, projecting the compositional vision into and unto the material world. The age-old reproof of art as an escape from life was here met with the means of art itself. The cyclic changes of sunlight and shadow and the man-made light patterns of electricity replaced line and pigment as painterly means. This had started very early and very unconsciously with the metal and glass constructions from 1921 and 1922, and it reached its fulfillment in the *Lichtrequisit* (literally light prop) constructed between 1922 and 1930. The original intention had been to project the interweaving high lights, shadows, black contours, and white framed fields on to a blank wall. The machine producing this interplay was a four foot high composition of rods, screens, flags, spheres, turned by a motor in a clearly visible gear arrangement. But there was no display space that would permit a permanent lightplay performance. So Moholy decided to make a film — *Lightplay Black-White-Gray* — which now seems almost like the cardiogram of his creative heart. In continuous motion the *Lightmachine* registered the finest gradations, the deepest space-creating superimpositions for which he had sought in his paintings. He had achieved a painterly-sculptural light composition whose kinetic principle created a totally new environmental relationship between the work of art and the man-made space that contains it.

■ With this the third and ultimate phase of Moholy's work becomes evident. Whatever the light-shadow variations might be they all derive from the eight years of light display apprenticeship — on plexiglas space modulators, in free-standing warped and incised plastic shapes, on "leaf paintings" of spiral-bound celluloid permitting the spectator to compose his own superimpositions, and in the ultimate fulfillment of the turning and stationary plexiglas sculptures executed between 1944 and 1946. These transparent forms were cut from one sheet and moulded under heat. Their main achievement is an interplay of inside-outside surfaces which form superimpositions of planes in the eye of the beholder, just as the chromatic over-lays of the second phase had done. Shape is a containment of depth, the transparent volume curving toward the infinite spaces surrounding every object. With these last pieces Moholy had seemingly gone back to the authors of the *Realistic Manifesto* who had proclaimed a quarter of a century earlier:

We reject in sculpture mass as a sculptural element. We restore line as direction to sculpture. We affirm depth to be the sole form of space in sculpture.[8]

But it is a superficial accord. The difference, in historical and personal development, is far deeper. The Manifesto had rejected the delineative value of line, assailing "the outline as an element of graphic illustration" with the same fervor with which it had rejected "color as the idealized optical face of objects." The sculptures of Gabo and Pevsner retained the beauty and the limitations of their pure linearity unchanged throughout forty years. They never went beyond the initial statement. Moholy's sculptures fall into two periods: the early ones in which space still depends on line as did his drawings and paintings; and the later ones, from the last 6 years of his life (1940—1946), where he has arrived at a sublimation and integration of the outline. A beam of light travels along the cut edges of the plexiglas sheet, at once part of and delineation of the moulded shapes that are of great variety. Without this delineative luminous edge, the transparent planes would dissolve into the accidental background of spaces and objects that make up physical environment.

■ In the last pieces of 1946 the need for mechanical mobility as in the *Lightmachine,* or the hand-worked girations of the suspended *Mobile with Chromium Rods,* had become redundant. In the unity of inside-outside curve, articulated by constantly alive reflections, statics and dynamics, line and plane, reflection and absorption, had become one.

■ The practical ramification of Moholy's core concep-

tions cannot be accommodated in a single exhibition. In his last book[9] he gave a full account of these extrapolations from his deepest commitment to his art, in stage design, film, photography, typography, graphics, and product research. Every cross-current was tested in the workshop curriculum of the Institute of Design (Chicago 1938—1946). Teaching to Moholy was profession in the original meaning of "to give testimony." His method has lost nothing of its appeal to young people in 25 years.

■ In Schiller's *Don Carlos* occurs the beautiful phrase: *"...and tell him that he must honour the dreams of his youth when he has become a man."*
The dream of Constructivism was "participation in life" — a celebration of the infinite wealth of vision in motion through the mastery of
space and line
color and superimposition
light and kinetics
freed of the accidental labels of "art" and "design."
Few men are granted the privilege and the strength to honor the dreams of their youth. Moholy-Nagy was one of them.

[1] Moholy-Nagy, Sibyl. *Moholy-Nagy, Experiment in Totality* Cambridge, 1969.
[2] Moholy-Nagy, Laszlo and L. Kássak. "Constructivist Manifesto," *Ma,* Vienna, 1921. (First publication; various versions later published.)
[3] Letter written in June 1934 and published in *Telehor,* Brno 1936.
[4] Mátyàs, Peter. *Horizont* 2, Ma, Vienna, 1921.
[5] Quoted by Paul Valery in *Variety,* New York, 1927.
[6] Moscow, August 1920. New translation by Camilla Gray in *The Structurist* 8, Saskatoon, 1968.
[7] *The New Vision,* Wittenborn & Co., New York, 1947. (Fourth revised edition.)
[8] *op. cit.*
[9] Moholy-Nagy, Laszlo. *Vision in Motion,* Paul Theobald Chicago, 1947.

Illustrations

Colored Segments, 1922/23 (cat. no. 93)

Large Emotion Meter, 1920 (cat. no. 5)

Large Railway Painting, 1920 (cat. no. 6)

Study for Architecture # 1, ca. 1920 (cat. no. 89)

Em I (Telephone Picture), 1922 (cat. no. 7)

A X I, 1923 (cat. no. 15)

Design for Light Machine for Total Theatre, 1922
(cat. no. 94)

Light-Space Modulator, 1921−30 (cat. no. 120)

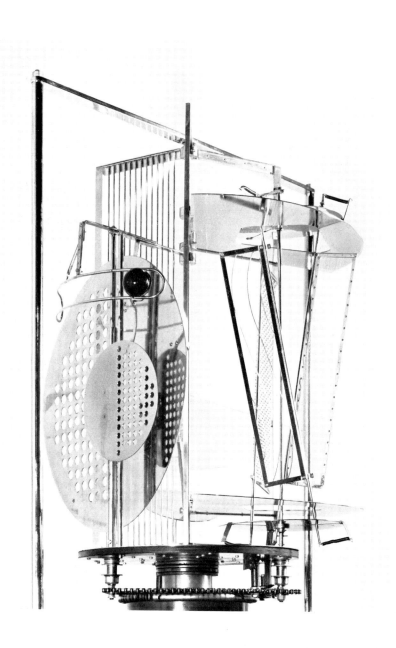

A L II, 1926 (cat. no. 23)

A X L II, 1927 (cat. no. 25)

La Sarraz, 1932 (cat. no. 27)

Abstraction, 1923—28 (cat. no. 80)

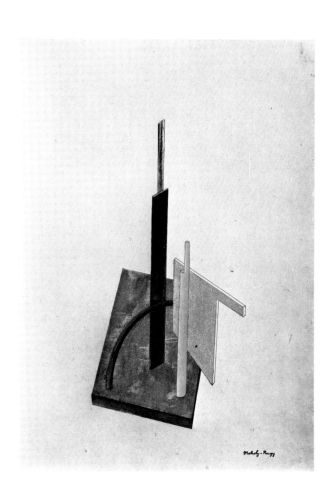

Space Modulator L 3, 1936 (cat. no. 28)

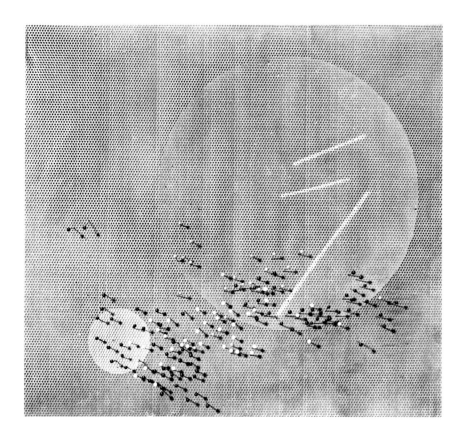

Mills No. 2, 1940 (cat. no. 45)

Space Modulator, 1938—40 (cat. no. 35)

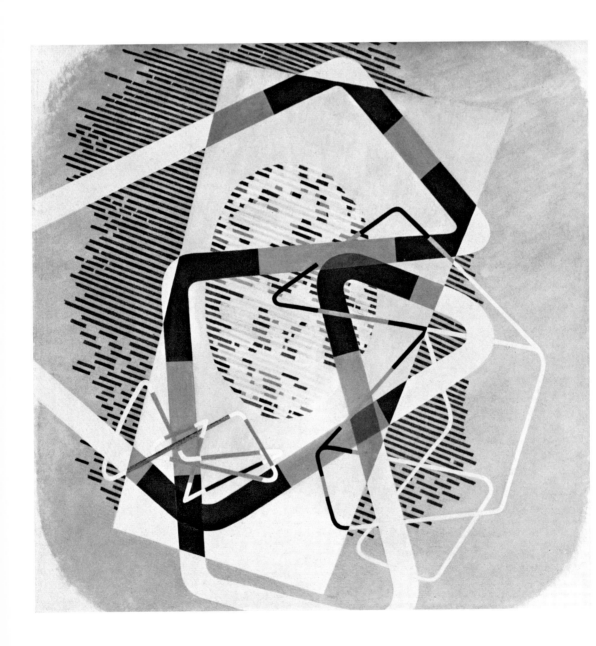

CH Beata I, 1939 (cat. no. 36)

L & C H, 1936—39 (cat. no. 30)

Composition, 1942 (cat. no. 55)

Leuk 4, 1945 (cat. no. 64)

Space Modulator, 1939—45 (cat. no. 42)

Space Modulator, 1945 (cat. no. 122)

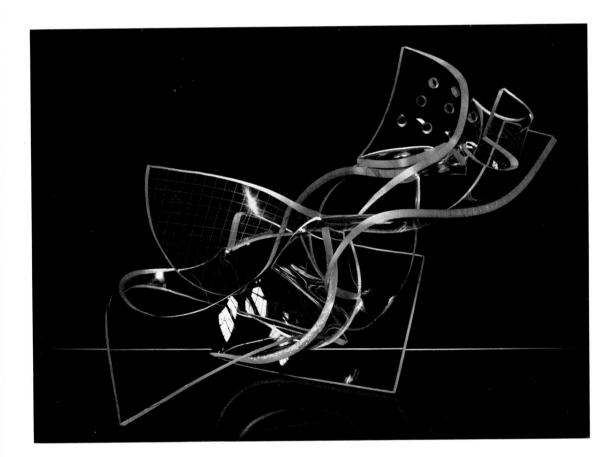

Light Modulator, 1943 (cat. no. 121)

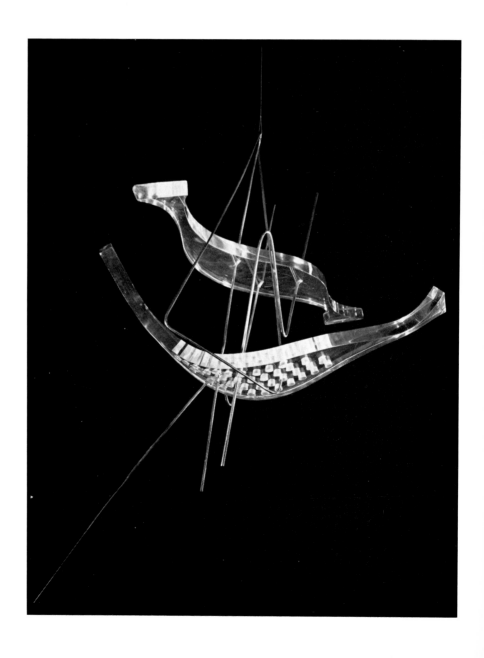

Loop, 1946 (cat. no. 124)

Space Modulator — Red over Black, 1946 (cat. no. 65)

Double Loop, 1946 (cat. no. 125)

Wire Curve, 1946 (cat. no. 123)

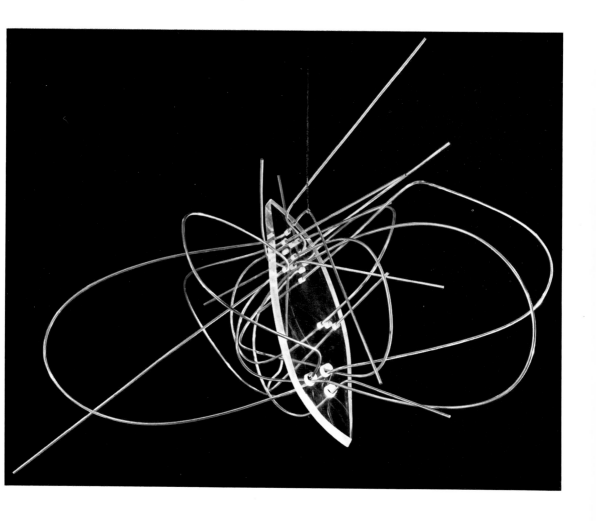

Ink in Motion, 1946 (cat. no. 112)

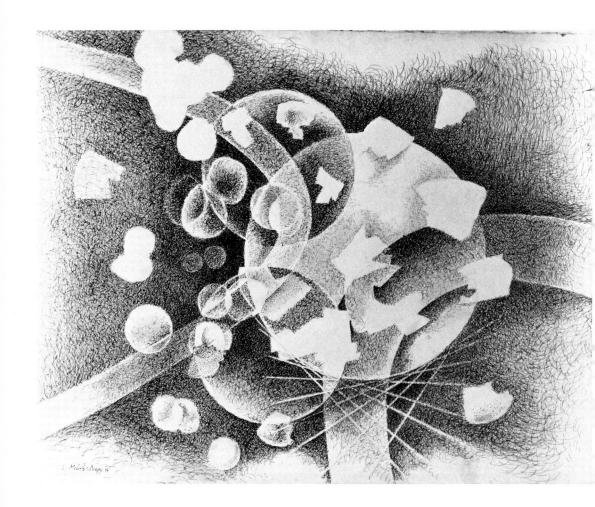

Leu # I, 1946 (cat. no. 68)

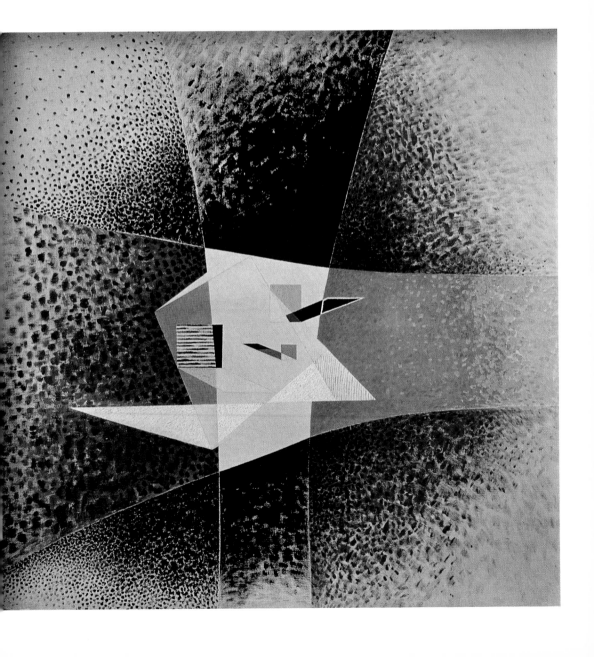

Selected Bibliography

Books by the Artist

- *Buch Neuer Künstler* (with L. Kássak), Ma, Vienna, 1922.
- *Die Bühne im Bauhaus* (with Oskar Schlemmer and Farkas Molnar), A. Langen, Munich, 1925 (Bauhausbücher 4). (Facsimile edition, Florian Kupferberg, Mainz and Berlin, 1964; translated as *The Theater of the Bauhaus*, Wesleyan University Press, Middletown, Conn., 1961, with an introduction by Walter Gropius.)
- *Malerei, Fotografie, Film*, A. Langen, Munich, 1925 (Bauhausbücher 8). (Facsimile edition with a postscript by Otto Stelzer, Florian Kupferberg, Mainz and Berlin, 1967; translated as *Painting, Photography, Film*, London, 1968.)
- *Von Material zu Architektur*, A. Langen, Munich, 1929 (Bauhausbücher 14). (Facsimile edition with a postscript by Otto Stelzer, Florian Kupferberg, Mainz and Berlin, 1968; translated as *The New Vision, From Material to Architecture*, Brewer, Warren & Putnam, New York, 1930; second edition, W. W. Norton, New York, 1938; third and subsequent editions with *Abstract of an Artist*, George Wittenborn, Inc., New York, 1946, 1947, 1964.)
- *Vision in Motion*, Paul Theobald, Chicago, 1947 (seventh printing 1964).

Articles and Statements by the Artist

- *Dynamo-Konstruktives Kräftesystem* (Manifesto der kinetischen Plastik, with A. Kémèny), Galerie Der Sturm, Berlin, 1922.
- "Zeitgemässe Typographie – Ziele, Praxis, Kritik," *Gutenberg Festschrift*, Gutenberg Gesellschaft, Mainz 1925.
- Editorial statement, *Offset-, Buch-, und Werbekunst*, Bauhaus Heft 7, Leipzig, 1926.
- "Die Beispiellose Fotografie," *i 10 Internationale Revue* 1:3:114–17, Amsterdam, 1927.
- "Fotografie ist Lichtgestaltung," *Bauhaus* 2:1:2–9, Dessau, 1928.
- "Confession," *The Little Review* 12:2, New York, May 1929.
- "La Photographie ce qu'elle était, ce qu'elle devra être," *Cahiers d'Art* 4:1:28–33, Paris, 1929.
- "The Future of the Photographic Process," *Transition* 15:289–293, Paris, February 1929.
- "Problèmes du nouveau film," *Cahiers d'Art* 7:6–7:277–80, Paris, 1932 (reprinted in *Telehor*, Brno, 1936).
- "How Photography Revolutionizes Vision," *The Listener*, London, November 8, 1933, 688–90 (reprinted in *Telehor*, Brno, 1936).
- "Offener Brief an die Filmindustrie und an Alle, die Interesse an der Entwicklung des guten Films haben," *Ekran* 1:1:13–15, Brno, November 15, 1934.
- "Photography in a Flash," *Industrial Arts* 1:294–303, London, Winter 1936.
- "Light-Architecture," *Industrial Arts* 1:15–17, London, Spring 1936.
- "Subject without Art," *The Studio* 12:259, New York, November 4, 1936.
- "Modern Art and Architecture," *Journal of the Royal Institute of British Architects* 44:210–13, London, January 9, 1937.
- "Moholy-Nagy, Picture Hunter, Looks at the Paris Exposition," *Architectural Record* 82:92–93, New York, October 1937.
- "Light Painting," *Circle, International Survey of Constructive Art*, (J. L. Martin, Ben Nicholson, N. Gabo, Eds.), London, 1937.

- "The New Bauhaus and Space Relationship," *American Architect and Architecture* 151:22—28, New York, December 1937.
- Introduction to Katherine Dreier's *1 to 40 Variations,* Springfield, Mass., 1937.
- "Richtlijnen voor een onbelemmerde kleurenfotografie," *Prisma der Kunsten,* Zeist, 1937, 100—105 (special issue *Foto '37*).
- "Why Bauhaus Education," *Shelter* 3:6—21, New York, March 1938.
- "Education and the Bauhaus," *Focus* 2:20—27, London, Winter 1938.
- "From Wine Jugs to Lighting Fixtures," *Bauhaus 1919—1928,* (W. Gropius, H. Bayer, I. Gropius, Eds.), Museum of Modern Art, New York, 1938.
- "New Approach to Fundamentals of Design," *More Business* 3:11:4—6, Chicago, November 1938 (special issue designed by Moholy-Nagy).
- "The New Bauhaus, American School of Design, Chicago," *Design* 40:19—21, Columbus, Ohio, March 1939.
- "Light a New Medium of Expression," *Architectural Forum* 70:44—48, Chicago, May 1939.
- "Painting with Light — A New Medium of Expression," *The Penrose Annual* 41:25—31, London, 1939.
- "Objectives of a Designer Education," *Conference on the Expansion of Industrial Communities with Regard to Housing and City Planning,* University of Michigan, College of Architecture and Design, Ann Arbor, 1940.
- "About the Elements of Motion Picture," *Design* 42:13, 24, Columbus, Ohio, October 1940.
- Design in Modern Theory and Practice," *California Arts and Architecture* 58:21, 35—36, Los Angeles, February 1941.
- "New Trends in Design," *Task* 1:27—31, New York, Summer 1941.
- "Education in Various Arts and Media for the Designer," *Art in American Life and Education* (Symposium), National Society for the Study of Education, Bloomington, Illinois, 1941.
- "Space-time and the Photographer," *American Annual of Photography 1943,* 57:7—14, Boston, 1942.
- "New Trends in Design," *Interiors* 102:48—51, New York, April 1943.
- "Better than Before," *The Technology Review* 46:1: 3—8, M.I.T., Cambridge, Mass., November 1943.
- "Design Potentialities," *New Architecture and City Planning: A Symposium,* (Paul Zucker, Ed.), Philosophical Library, New York, 1944.
- "Photography in the Study of Design," *American Annual of Photography 1945,* 59:158—64, Boston, 1944.
- "On Art and the Photograph," *The Technology Review* 47:8:491—94, 518, 520, 522, M.I.T., Cambridge, Mass., June 1945.
- "In Defense of Abstract Art," *Journal of Aesthetics and Art Criticism* IV:74—76, Cleveland, 1945.
- "Space-Time Problems in Art," *The World of Abstract Art,* American Abstract Artists, New York, 1946.
- "Design Education," *Architectural Review* 99:32—33, London, January 1946.
- "New Education — Organic Approach," *Art and Industry* 40:66—77, London, March 1946.
- "Art in Industry," *Arts and Architecture* 64:30, Los Angeles, September 1947; 64:28, October 1947.

Published Photographs and Illustrations by the Artist

Films by the Artist

- *Moholy-Nagy. 60 Fotos,* (Franz Roh, Ed.), Berlin, 1930.
- *The Street Market of London* (with Mary Benedetta), London, 1936.
- *Eton Portrait* (with Bernard Fergusson), London, 1937.
- *An Oxford University Chest,* by John Betjeman, London, 1939.

- Dynamik der Groszstadt, 1921.
- Berliner Stilleben, 1926.
- Marseille Vieux Port, 1929.
- Once a chicken, always a chicken, 1925–30.
- Lichtspiel schwarz-weiss-grau, 1930.
- Tönender ABC, 1932.
- Zigeuner, 1932.
- Architekturkongress Athen, 1933.
- Street Picture, Finland, 1933.
- Life of the Lobster, 1935.
- The New Architecture at the London Zoo, 1936.

General Works on the Artist

■ *Architectural Forum* 67:22, 82, "The New Bauhaus," Chicago, October 1937.
■ Banham, Reyner. *Theory and Design in the First Machine Age,* London and New York, 1960.
■ Blesh, Rudi and Janis, Harriet. *Collage*, Philadelphia and New York, 1962.
■ Branford, Charles T. *Bauhaus, Weimar 1919–25, Dessau 1925–38,* Boston, 1952.
■ Bredendieck, Hin, "The Legacy of the Bauhaus," *Art Journal* 22:1:15–21, New York, Fall 1962.
■ Brion, Marcel. *Art Abstrait,* Paris, 1956.
■ Burnham, Jack. *Beyond Modern Sculpture*, New York, 1968.
■ Fenton, Terry. "Two Contributions to the Art and Science Muddle: I. Constructivism and Its Confusions," *Artforum* 7:22–27, New York, January 1969.
■ Frost, Rosamund. "Form and Function: A U. S. Bauhaus," *Art News* 44:23, New York, August 1945.
■ Giedion, Siegfried. *Walter Gropius, Work and Teamwork,* New York, 1954.
■ Giedion-Welcker, Carola. *Contemporary Sculpture. An Evolution in Volume and Space,* third edition, New York, 1960.
■ Grohmann, Will. "L'art non-figuratif en Allemagne," *L'Amour de l'Art,* Paris, 1934, 433–37.
■ —. "Art into Architecture: The Bauhaus Ethos," *Apollo* 76:37–41, London, March 1962.
■ —. Introductory essay, *Painters of the Bauhaus,* Marlborough Fine Arts, London, 1962.
■ Gropius, Walter. *Idee und Aufbau des Staatlichen Bauhauses Weimar,* Munich, 1923.
■ —. *The New Architecture and the Bauhaus,* Cambridge, Mass., 1935 (book cover by Moholy-Nagy).
■ Gropius, Walter, with Herbert Bayer and Ise Gropius, Eds. *Bauhaus 1919–1928,* Museum of Modern Art, New York, 1938 (second edition, Boston, 1952).
■ Grote, Ludwig. "Les Peintres du 'Bauhaus'," *Art d'Aujourd'hui* 4:4–5, Paris, August 1953.
■ Haftmann, Werner. *Malerei im 20. Jahrhundert,* Munich, 1954.

■ Hill, Anthony. "Constructivism – the European Phenomenon," *Studio International* 171:140–47, London, April 1966.
■ Hitchcock, Henry-Russell. *Painting Toward Architecture,* New York, 1948.
■ Hofmann, Werner. *Die Plastik des 20. Jahrhunderts,* Frankfurt am Main, 1958.
■ Huyghe, René and Bazin, Germaine (Eds.). *Histoire de l'Art Contemporain, La Peinture,* Paris, 1935 (entry by Will Grohmann).
■ Hultén, K. G. P. *The Machine as Seen at the End of the Mechanical Age,* The Museum of Modern Art, New York, 1968.
■ Irwin, David. "Motion and the Sorcerer's Apprentice," *Apollo* 84:54–61, London, July 1966.
■ Kállai, Ernst. *Neue Malerei in Ungarn,* Leipzig, 1925 (volume 2 of *Die Junge Kunst in Europa*).
■ *Knaurs Lexikon der Modernen Kunst,* Munich, 1961.
■ *Knaurs Lexikon der Modernen Plastik,* Munich, 1961.
■ Kozloff, Max. "A Confusion in Buffalo. 'Plus by Minus' rather amounts to less ...," *Artforum* 6:50–53, New York, May 1968.
■ Kramer, Hilton. "Engineers of Esthetic Sensation," *New York Times,* June 23, 1968.
■ Moholy-Nagy, Sibyl. "Constructivism from Malevitch to Moholy-Nagy," *Arts and Architecture* 83:27–28, Los Angeles, June 1966.
■ Myers, Bernard. "The Bauhaus – Graphic Design," *Studio International* 176:100–107, London, September 1968.
■ Naylor, Gillian. *The Bauhaus,* London, 1968.
■ Neumann, E. *Bauhaus and Bauhaus Teachers,* New York, 1968.
■ Orso, Martino dell. "A la recherche d'une synthèse de la forme et du mouvement," *Age Nouveau* 9:23–32, Paris, 1955.
■ Pearson, Ralph M. "The School of Design, The American Bauhaus," *The New Art Education,* New York, 1941.

Specific Articles, Catalogues, Monographs, Reviews on the Artist

■ Piene, Nan R. "Light Art," *Art in America* 55:3:24—47, New York, May-June 1967. (Includes English translation of filmscript "Lichtspiel schwarz-weiss-grau.")
■ Read, Herbert. "Abstract Art: A note for the uninitiated," *Axis* 5:3—19, Spring 1936.
■ —. *A Concise History of Modern Sculpture,* New York, 1964.
■ Rickey, George. "The Morphology of Movement, A Study of Kinetic Art," *Art Journal* 22:220—231, New York, Summer 1963.
■ —. *Constructivism. Origins and Evolution,* New York, 1967.
■ Scheidig, Walter. *Crafts of the Weimar Bauhaus,* London, 1967.
■ Schreyer, Lothar. *Erinnerungen an Sturm und Bauhaus: Was ist des Menschen Bild?,* Munich, 1956.
■ Seuphor, Michel. *L'Art abstrait, ses origines, ses premiers maîtres,* Paris, 1949.
■ —. *Dictionnaire de la Peinture Abstraite,* Paris, 1957.
■ —. *The Sculpture of this Century,* New York, 1960.
■ —. "Art construit," *XXe Siècle* 24:23, Paris, June 1962.
■ Shand, P. M. "New Eyes for Old," *Architectural Review* 75:11—12, London, January 1934.
■ Spear, Athena Tacha. "Sculptured Light," *Art International* XI/10:29—49, Lugano, Christmas 1967.
■ Thieme & Becker (Eds.). *Allgemeines Lexikon der Bildenden Künstler* 25:19—20, Leipzig, 1931 (entry by Will Grohmann).
■ Vollmer, Hans. *Allgemeines Lexikon der Bildenden Künstler des XX. Jahrhunderts* 3:408, Leipzig, 1953—61.
■ Wingler, Hans Maria. *Das Bauhaus,* Osnabrück, 1963 (English translation, Cambridge, Mass., 1969).

■ *Art and Industry* 22:110—15, "Moholy-Nagy, Experimentalist," London, March 1937.
■ *Art News* 56:16, "Reviews and Previews," New York, October 1957 (Fairfield Porter).
■ Coolidge, John (Ed.). *Works of Art by Moholy-Nagy,* Cambridge, Fogg Art Museum, 1950.
■ Cuijel, Hans. "Moholy-Nagy und das Theater," *Du* 24:11—15, Zurich, November 1964.
■ Dorner, Alexander. "Laszlo Moholy-Nagy," *Nueva Vision* 7:11—19, Buenos Aires, 1955.
■ Erfurth, Hugo. "Moholy-Nagy," *Qualität. Zeitschrift für Ware und Werbung* 9:1—2, 8, Dessau, 1931 (cover design by Moholy-Nagy).
■ Fry, E. Maxwell. Introductory essay, *Moholy-Nagy,* New London Gallery, London, 1961.
■ Giedion, Siegfried. Introductory essay, *L. Moholy-Nagy,* New London Gallery, London, 1937.
■ —. "Laszlo Moholy-Nagy," *Metron* 13:12—14, Rome, 1946.
■ —. "Notes on the Life and Work of Laszlo Moholy-Nagy, Painter-Universalist," *Architects' Year Book* 3:32—35, London, 1949.
■ —. "The Work of Laszlo Moholy-Nagy," Kleemann Galleries, New York, 1957.
■ Gropius, Walter. "Laszlo Moholy-Nagy, 1895—1946," *Collection of the Société Anonyme,* Yale University Art Gallery, New Haven, 1950.
■ Hess, Thomas B. "Memorial to a Many-Sided Non-Objectivist," *Art News* 46:22—23, 49, 50, New York, June 1947.
■ *Interiors* 107:88—91, "Moholy Took Pen in Hand," New York, 1948.
■ Kalivoda, Fr., Ed. *Telehor,* Brno, 1936. (Special issue devoted to Moholy-Nagy includes a foreword by Siegfried Giedion, postscript by Fr. Kalivoda, a letter from Moholy-Nagy to Kalivoda and the following writings by Moholy-Nagy: "From Pigment to Light," 1923—26; "A New Instrument of Vision," 1932; "Problems of the Modern Film," 1928—30; Supplementary Remarks on the Sound and Colour Film," 1935; "Once a chicken, always a chicken," 1925—30.)

■ Kállai, Ernst. "Ladislaus Moholy-Nagy," *Jahrbuch der Jungen Kunst* 5:181—89, Leipzig, 1924.
■ Kaufmann, Edgar, Jr. "Moholy," *Arts and Architecture* 64:25, Los Angeles, March 1947.
■ Kovacs, Istvan. "Totality through Light — the Work of Laszlo Moholy-Nagy," *Form* 6:14—19, Cambridge, England, December 1967.
■ Kuh, Katherine. "Moholy-Nagy in Chicago," *L. Moholy-Nagy,* The Art Institute of Chicago, Chicago, 1947.
■ Martin, J. L. "Laszlo Moholy-Nagy and the Chicago Institute of Design," *Architectural Review* 101:224—26, London, June 1947.
■ Mátyás, Peter, Ed. *Horizont 2,* Ma, Vienna, 1921.
■ Moholy-Nagy, Sibyl. "Documented Seeing," *Art and Photography,* Chicago, 1949.
■ —. "The Making of a Constructivist," *Copy* 1:1, San Francisco, January 1950.
■ —. *Moholy-Nagy, Experiment in Totality,* New York, 1950 (second edition, Cambridge, Mass., 1969).
■ —. "Laszlo Moholy-Nagy," *Art d'Aujourd'hui* 2:8: 19—25, Paris, October 1951.
■ —. "Moholy-Nagy und die Idee des Konstruktivismus," *Die Kunst und Das Schöne Heim* 57:9:330—33, Munich, June 1959.
■ Newhall, Beaumont. "The Photography of Moholy-Nagy," *The Kenyon Review* 3:344—51, Gambier, Ohio, Summer 1941.
■ Read, Herbert. "A New Humanism," *The Architectural Review* 78:150—51, London, October 1935 (review of *The New Vision*).
■ Rebay, Hilla. "Moholy-Nagy the Painter and Friend," *In Memoriam Laszlo Moholy-Nagy,* The Solomon R. Guggenheim Foundation, New York, 1947.
■ Reichardt, Jasia. "Moholy-Nagy at New London Gallery," *Apollo* 74:206, London, June 1961.
■ —. "Moholy-Nagy and light art as an art of the future," Studio International 174:894:184—85, London, November 1967.

■ *Schniewind, Carl O.* "Moholy-Nagy," *L. Moholy-Nagy,* The Art Institute of Chicago, Chicago, 1949.
■ Weitemeier, Hannah. "Vision in Motion," *Moholy-Nagy,* Stedelijk van Abbemuseum, Eindhoven, 1967.

No attempt at inclusiveness has been made. A complete bibliography of the writings by and on Moholy-Nagy is as yet non-existent.

Works in the Exhibition

Paintings

1. Brücken
1919
Oil on canvas
$37^1/_2$ x $27^7/_8$"
Saarland Museum, Saarbrucken

2. Yellow Disc
1919/20
Oil on canvas
26 x 20"
Jewett Arts Center, Wellesley, Massachusetts,
Gift of Mrs. Sibyl Moholy-Nagy

3. The Bicyclist
1920
Oil on canvas
$37^1/_2$ x $29^3/_4$"
Carlos Raúl Villanueva, Caracas

4. Architecture #1
1920
Oil on canvas
$25^1/_2$ x $21^1/_2$"
Private Collection, New York

5. Large Emotion Meter
1920
Oil on canvas
$37^1/_2$ x $29^1/_2$"
Stedelijk van Abbemuseum, Eindhoven

6. Large Railway Painting
1920
Oil on canvas
$39^3/_8$ x 30"
Mr. and Mrs. Fred Shore, New York

7. Em 1 (Telephone Picture)
1922
Porcelain enamel on steel
$37^1/_2$ x 24"
Private Collection, Chicago

8. Em 2 (Telephone Picture)
1922
Porcelain enamel on steel
$18^3/_4$ x $11^7/_8$"
Philip Johnson, New York

9. Em 3 (Telephone Picture)
1922
Porcelain enamel on steel
$9^1/_2$ x 6"
Philip Johnson, New York

10. K 1
1922
Oil on canvas
30 x $37^1/_2$
Smith College Museum of Art,
Northampton, Massachusetts

11. Z III
1922
Oil on canvas
$37^3/_4$ x $29^3/_4$"
Marlborough-Gerson Gallery, New York

12. Z IV
1923
Oil on canvas
$37^1/_2$ x $30^1/_2$"
Galerie Klihm, Munich

13. A 5 ("Mein buntes Bild")
1923
Oil on canvas
29 x 38"
Mrs. Sibyl Moholy-Nagy, New York

14. A VIII
1923
Oil on canvas
$37^1/_2$ x $30^1/_2$"
Galerie Klihm, Munich

15. A X I
1923
Oil on canvas
53 x 46"
Mrs. Sibyl Moholy-Nagy, New York

16. Q XXI
1923
Oil on canvas
7 x 30"
New York University Art Collection,
Gift of Miss Silvia Pizitz
17. C XVI
1923
Oil on canvas
40½ x 33"
Mrs. Sibyl Moholy-Nagy, New York
18. C XII
1924
Oil on canvas
36 x 28"
Mrs. Sibyl Moholy-Nagy, New York
19. AM 2
1925
Oil on canvas
37¾ x 29⅝"
Lillian H. Florshiem Foundation for Fine Arts, Chicago
20. G 7a
1925
Oil on galalith
15¾ x 20¼"
Walter Gropius, South Lincoln, Massachusetts
21. G 8
1926
Oil on galalith
16 x 19⅞"
Mrs. Sibyl Moholy-Nagy, New York
22. T 1
1926
Oil on bakelite
55 x 24⅜"
The Solomon R. Guggenheim Museum, New York
23. A L II
1926
Oil on aluminum
31¾ x 38¾"
Mrs. Sibyl Moholy-Nagy, New York

24. A 19
1927
Oil on canvas
23½ x 37½"
Mrs. Sibyl Moholy-Nagy, New York
25. AXL II
1927
Oil on canvas
37⅛ x 29⅛"
The Solomon R. Guggenheim Museum, New York,
Gift of Mr. and Mrs. Andrew Fuller, New York, 1964
26. Tp 2
1930
Oil on bakelite
24¼ x 56¾"
The Solomon R. Guggenheim Museum, New York
27. La Sarraz
1932
Oil on canvas
18 x 12"
Kovler Gallery, Chicago
28. Space Modulator L 3
1936
Perforated zinc over oil on composition board
with glass headed pins
17¼ x 19⅛"
The Museum of Modern Art, New York
29. LK IIII
1936
Oil on canvas
37½ x 30"
Mrs. Sibyl Moholy-Nagy, New York
30. L & CH
1936—39
Oil on canvas
38 x 30"
Marlborough-Gerson Gallery, New York
31. Kupferbild
1937
Oil on copper
20 x 26"
Bauhaus-Archiv, Darmstadt

32. CH 3
1938
Oil on canvas
50 x 39¹/₂"
Mrs. Sibyl Moholy-Nagy, New York
33. CH 3 A 1
1938
Oil and engraving on aluminum
12 x 12"
Mr. and Mrs. Edward Druzinsky, Chicago
34. CH 4
1938
Oil on canvas
27 x 35¹/₂"
Mrs. Sibyl Moholy-Nagy, New York
35. Space Modulator
1938—40
Oil on canvas
47 x 47"
Whitney Museum of American Art, New York
Gift of Mrs. Sibyl Moholy-Nagy
36. CH Beata 1
1939
Oil on canvas
47¹/₈ x 47¹/₈"
The Solomon R. Guggenheim Museum, New York
37. CH 8
1939
30 x 38"
Oil on canvas
Mrs. Claudia Imlay, Santa Monica, California
38. CH X
1939
Oil on canvas
30¹/₄ x 38¹/₈"
The Solomon R. Guggenheim Museum, New York
39. CH XIV
1939
Oil on canvas
47 x 47"
Mrs. Sibyl Moholy-Nagy, New York

40. SIL 2
1939
Oil on silverit
19³/₄ x 23⁵/₈"
The Solomon R. Guggenheim Museum, New York
41. For CMN
1939
Oil on plexiglas
54³/₄ x 25"
Carlos Raúl Villanueva, Caracas
42. Space Modulator
1939—45
Oil on incised plaster
24⁷/₈ x 26"
The Solomon R. Guggenheim Museum, New York
43. CH 8 A
1940
Oil on canvas
36 x 26"
Mrs. Sibyl Moholy-Nagy, New York
44. Mills No. 1
1940
Oil on plexiglas
34⁵/₈ x 26"
The Solomon R. Guggenheim Museum, New York
45. Mills No. 2
1940
Oil on plexiglas
34⁷/₈ x 26"
The Solomon R. Guggenheim Museum, New York
46. CH 4
1941
Oil on plexiglas
35⁷/₈ x 35⁷/₈"
The Solomon R. Guggenheim Museum, New York
47. CH 7
1941
Oil on canvas
47¹/₈ x 47¹/₈"
The Solomon R. Guggenheim Museum, New York

48. CH B 3
1941
Oil on canvas
50 x 80"
The Solomon R. Guggenheim Museum, New York

49. CH B 4
1941
Oil on canvas
50^1/$_8$ x 40^1/$_4$"
The Solomon R. Guggenheim Museum, New York

50. Untitled
1941—46
Oil on canvas
12 x 9"
Mr. and Mrs. Leonard J. Horwich, Chicago

51. Sketch for Bennett Sculpture
1941—46
Oil on canvasboard
12 x 8^7/$_8$"
The Solomon R. Guggenheim Museum, New York

52. Tp 1
1942
Oil on bakelite
24 x 57"
The Solomon R. Guggenheim Museum, New York

53. Space Modulator
1942
Oil on formica
61 x 24"
Mrs. Sibyl Moholy-Nagy, New York

54. Space Modulator
("Scene from my Lightplay")
1942
Oil on formica
61 x 24"
Mrs. Sibyl Moholy-Nagy, New York

55. Composition
1942
Oil on incised plexiglas
22^1/$_2$ x 17^1/$_4$"
Marlborough-Gerson Gallery, New York

56. Prehistoric Construction
1942
Oil on incised plexiglas
10 x 24^7/$_8$"
The Solomon R. Guggenheim Museum, New York

57. Papmac
1943
Oil on plexiglas
23 x 28"
Carlos Raúl Villanueva, Caracas

58. Space Modulator CH 1
1943
Acrylic on canvas
50 x 40^1/$_4$"
Mr. and Mrs. Arthur Siegel, Chicago

59. Space Modulator (The Ovale)
1943—45
Oil on plexiglas
36 x 24"
The Solomon R. Guggenheim Museum, New York

60. Space Modulator
1945
Oil on incised plexiglas
18 x 12"
The Solomon R. Guggenheim Museum, New York

61. Space Modulator with Yellow Aura
1945
Oil on plexiglas
36 x 24"
The Solomon R. Guggenheim Museum, New York

62. Zweiton
1945
Oil on plexiglas
18 x 24"
Mrs. Sibyl Moholy-Nagy, New York

63. The Ovals
1945
Oil on canvas
38^1/$_8$ x 30^1/$_4$"
The Solomon R. Guggenheim Museum, New York

Collages

64. Leuk 4
1945
Oil on canvas
49 x 49^1/$_8$"
The Solomon R. Guggenheim Museum, New York
65. Space Modulator – Red over Black
1946
Oil on plexiglas with screening
18^1/$_8$ x 25^1/$_2$"
The Detroit Institute of Arts
66. Nuclear II
1946
Oil on canvas
49^1/$_4$ x 49^1/$_4$"
Mr. and Mrs. Kenneth Parker, Janesville, Wisconsin
67. Space (Nuclear) Green
1946
Oil on canvas
38^1/$_4$ x 30^1/$_8$"
The Solomon R. Guggenheim Museum, New York
68. Leu #1
1946
Oil on canvas
50 x 50"
Mrs. Walter Paepcke, Chicago
69. CHI-Finis
1946
Oil on canvas
50 x 80"
The Solomon R. Guggenheim Museum, New York

70. Collage R
1920
Watercolor and collage on paper
25^3/$_4$ x 18^1/$_4$
George M. Irwin, Quincy, Illinois
72. Überschneidung
1921
Collage on paper
12^1/$_2$ x 7^1/$_2$"
Mrs. Sibyl Moholy-Nagy, New York
72. Rotes Klebebild
1921
Collage on paper
9^1/$_2$ x 13^1/$_2$"
Mrs. Sibyl Moholy-Nagy, New York
73. 25 Pleitegeier
1922
12^3/$_4$ x 10"
Mrs. Sibyl Moholy-Nagy, New York
74. Untitled
1922
Collage on paper
26^1/$_2$ x 19^1/$_4$
Stedelijk van Abbemuseum, Eindhoven
75. Collage with Red Segment on Grey Background
1922
Collage on paper
32 x 26"
Mrs. Sibyl Moholy-Nagy, New York
76. Blaues und schwarzes Kreuz mit Bleistiftlinien
1922
Collage on paper
17^3/$_4$ x 11^1/$_2$"
Stedelijk van Abbemuseum, Eindhoven
77. Untitled
ca. 1922
India ink and collage on paper
10^3/$_4$ x 8^1/$_2$"
Mrs. Sibyl Moholy-Nagy, New York

Drawings

78. à Helène par aventure
1923
Collage on paper
18¹/₂ x 12¹/₄"
Mrs. Sibyl Moholy-Nagy, New York

79. Entwurf Malevitch Umschlag
ca. 1923
Watercolor and collage on paper
20 x 13¹/₂"
Mrs. Sibyl Moholy-Nagy, New York

80. Abstraction
1923—28
Collage on paper
18³/₈ x 13"
Seattle Art Museum

81. Untitled
ca. 1925
Collage on paper
18 x 14"
Mrs. Sibyl Moholy-Nagy, New York

82. La Sarraz
1930
Collage and watercolor on paper
18³/₄ x 24³/₄"
The Solomon R. Guggenheim Museum, New York

83. Sand Disk
1941
Collage on paper
20 x 16"
Charles W. Niedringhaus, New York

84. Stacheldrahtlandschaft
1917
Crayon on paper
28 x 35"
Mrs. Sibyl Moholy-Nagy, New York

85. Frachthof
1917
Pencil on paper
20 x 27"
Mrs. Sibyl Moholy-Nagy, New York

86. Akos, my brother
ca. 1919
Pencil on paper
20 x 13¹/₂"
Mrs. Sibyl Moholy-Nagy, New York

87. Bridges
1920
Watercolor and india ink on paper
13 x 10"
Haags Gemeentemuseum, The Hague

88. Typographical Composition
1920
India ink on paper
8¹/₂ x 12"
Henry G. Proskauer, New York

89. Study for Architecture #1
ca. 1920
Watercolor on paper
9⁷/₈ x 7¹/₈"
Private Collection, New York

90. Self Portrait
ca. 1920
Crayon on paper
15³/₄ x 12¹/₄"
Mrs. Sibyl Moholy-Nagy, New York

91. Portrait Dr. Reinhold Scheyrer
1921
Crayon on paper
24¹/₄ x 19¹/₂"
Mrs. Sibyl Moholy-Nagy, New York

92. Untitled (superimposed)
ca. 1922
India ink on paper
12³/₄ x 10″
Mrs. Sibyl Moholy-Nagy, New York

93. Colored Segments
1922/23
Watercolor on paper
22 x 18″
Herron Museum of Art, Indianapolis,
Gift of Mr. and Mrs. James W. Alsdorf

94. Design for a Light Machine for Total Theatre
1922
Ink and tempera on paper
17³/₄ x 13″
Bauhaus-Archiv, Darmstadt

95. Die Mechanik des Lichtrequisits
1922–30
Watercolor and ink on masonite
∅ 20³/₄″
Mrs. Sibyl Moholy-Nagy, New York

96. XIX
1923
Tempera and india ink on paper
14³/₄ x 12¹/₂″
Mrs. Sibyl Moholy-Nagy, New York

97. Planes Cutting Planes
Before 1927
Gouache on paper
19⁷/₁₆ x 13⁵/₈″
Yale University Art Gallery, New Haven,
Collection Société Anonyme

98. Construction 1280
ca. 1927
Watercolor, pencil, and ink on paper
13¹/₂ x 20³/₈″
The Solomon R. Guggenheim Museum, New York

99. Composition
ca. 1927
Watercolor and ink on paper
11 x 15¹/₂″
The Solomon R. Guggenheim Museum, New York

100. Spiral
ca. 1932
Watercolor and ink on paper
27¹/₄ x 19⁷/₈″
The Solomon R. Guggenheim Museum, New York

101. Sketch for Bennett Sculpture
1943–46
Gouache and pencil on board
19⁵/₈ x 14⁷/₈″
The Solomon R. Guggenheim Museum, New York

102. Untitled
1944
Crayon and wood rubbing on paper
11 x 8¹/₂″
Mrs. Sibyl Moholy-Nagy, New York

103. Untitled
1944
Crayon and wood rubbing on paper
8¹/₂ x 11″
Mrs. Sibyl Moholy-Nagy, New York

104. Construction
1945
Tempera, watercolor, and ink on board
20 x 14⁷/₈″
The Solomon R. Guggenheim Museum, New York

105. Drawing
1945
Crayon on paper
10³/₄ x 8¹/₄″
George M. Irwin, Quincy, Illinois

106. Diary of a fly (dedicated to Bartók)
1946
Crayon and ink on paper
14¹/₄ x 18″
Mrs. Sibyl Moholy-Nagy, New York

Prints

107. Untitled
1946
Crayon and ink on paper
17 x 14¹/₄"
Mrs. Sibyl Moholy-Nagy, New York
108. CH (Summer)
1946
Crayon on paper
12 x 9"
Mrs. Sibyl Moholy-Nagy, New York
109. Untitled
1946
Ink and gouache on paper
17⁷/₈ x 14¹/₄"
The Solomon R. Guggenheim Museum, New York
110. Untitled
1946
Ink and chalk on paper
18 x 14¹/₈"
Bauhaus-Archiv, Darmstadt
111. Ink Drawing (B)
1946
Watercolor and ink on board
20 x 15"
The Solomon R. Guggenheim Museum, New York
112. Ink in Motion
1946
Ink on cardboard
29 x 37"
Mrs. Sibyl Moholy-Nagy, New York
113. Watercolor 2
1946
Gouache, ink, and pencil on paper
14¹/₄ x 18"
The Solomon R. Guggenheim Museum, New York
114. Watercolor 3
1946
Watercolor and ink on paper
14¹/₄ x 18"
The Solomon R. Guggenheim Museum, New York

115. Untitled
ca. 1922
Etching (1st proof)
11¹/₂ x 9¹/₂"
Mrs. Sibyl Moholy-Nagy, New York
116. Untitled
ca. 1922
Etching
8 x 10¹/₂"
Mrs. Sibyl Moholy-Nagy, New York
117. Untitled
ca. 1922
Etching
8 x 10¹/₂"
Mrs. Sibyl Moholy-Nagy, New York
118. Architektur
1923
Woodcut
11 x 10¹/₂"
Mrs. Sibyl Moholy-Nagy, New York
119. Konstruktionen
(Kestner portfolio No. 6, Copy No. 3/50)
1923
8 Lithographs
23³/₄ x 17⁵/₁₆" each
University Art Museum, University of California,
Berkeley

Sculptures

120. Light-Space Modulator
(Lichtrequisit)
1921–30
Mobile construction: steel, plastic, and wood
59$^1/_2$" h. with base
Busch-Reisinger Museum of Germanic Culture,
Cambridge, Massachusetts
121. Light Modulator
1943
Plexiglas and chrome plated steel rods
32$^3/_4$ x 23$^5/_8$"
Mr. and Mrs. Eugene A. Davidson, Chicago
122. Space Modulator
1945
Plexiglas
10$^3/_4$ x 16$^1/_2$ x 25"
The Detroit Institute of Arts
123. Wire Curve
1946
Plexiglas and chrome plated steel rods
36$^1/_2$ x 47$^7/_8$"
The Solomon R. Guggenheim Museum, New York
124. Loop
1946
Plexiglas
14$^1/_4$ x 18"
Carlos Raúl Villanueva, Caracas
125. Double Loop
1946
Plexiglas
16$^1/_4$ x 22$^1/_4$ x 17$^1/_2$"
The Museum of Modern Art, New York
126. The Spirals
1946
Plexiglas
19$^1/_2$ x 15 x 16"
Mrs. Sibyl Moholy-Nagy, New York
127. Leda and the Swan
1946
Plexiglas
22 x 16$^1/_4$ x 15$^3/_4$"
The Solomon R. Guggenheim Museum, New York

A representative group of photographs, photograms, stage and typographic designs will be presented as a corollary to this exhibition.

Photo Credits

The Art Institute of Chicago (b/w):
Light Modulator, cat. no. 121, p. 41

Oliver Baker Associates (b/w):
Space Modulator, cat. no. 35, p. 34

Franz Berko (color reproduction):
Leu # 1, cat. no. 68, p. 47

(b/w):
Design for a Light Machine for Total Theatre, cat. no. 94, p. 26

Busch-Reisinger Museum of Germanic Culture, Cambridge:
Light-Space Modulator, cat. no. 120, p. 27

The Detroit Institute of Arts (b/w):
Space Modulator — Red over Black, cat. no. 65, p. 43
Space Modulator, cat. no. 122, p. 40

Vories Fisher:
Frontispiece portrait, p. 9

The Solomon R. Guggenheim Museum (color reproductions):
(Robert E. Mates and Paul Katz)
CH Beata I, cat. no. 36, p. 35
Space Modulator, cat. no. 42, p. 39

(b/w):
A X L II, cat. no. 25, p. 29
Mills No. 2, cat. no. 45, p. 33
Wire Curve, cat. no. 123, p. 45
Leuk 4, cat. no. 64, p. 38

Herron Museum of Art (b/w):
Colored Segments, cat. no. 93, p. 20

Kovler Gallery (b/w):
La Sarraz, cat. no. 27, p. 30

Marlborough Fine Art (b/w):
Large Railway Painting, cat. no. 6, p. 22

Massachusetts Institute of Technology (b/w):
Loop, cat. no. 124, p. 42

The Museum of Modern Art (b/w):
   (Soichi Sunami)
   Space Modulator L 3, cat. no. 28, p. 32
   Double Loop, cat. no. 125, p. 44

O. E. Nelson (b/w):
   Composition, cat. no. 55, p. 37
   L & C H, cat. no. 30, p. 36

Walter Rosenblum (b/w):
   Study for Architecture # 1, cat. no. 89, p. 23

Seattle Art Museum (b/w):
   Abstraction, cat. no. 80, p. 31

F. van den Bichelaer (b/w):
   Large Emotion Meter, cat. no. 5, p. 21

David Van Riper (color reproductions):
   A X I, cat. no. 15, p. 25
   A L II, cat. no. 23, p. 28

   (b/w):
   Em I, cat. no. 7, p. 24
   Ink in Motion, cat. no. 112, p. 46

5,000 copies of this catalogue
designed by Arthur S. Congdon
have been printed by Brüder Hartmann, Berlin, in April 1969
on the occasion of the loan exhibition "Laszlo Moholy-Nagy."